Teaching the Craft of Writing

Leads & Endings

by Kathleen Hurni-Dove

New York • Toronto • London • Auckland • Sydney
Mexico City • New Delhi • Hong Kong • Buenos Aires

Teaching *Resources*

Dedication

To my husband, children, and grandchildren

Acknowledgments

A special thank you to the children and teachers at J.R. Watson Elementary School who shared their books, writing, and great conversation.

A very special thank you to Fort Wayne Community Schools Curriculum Department, students, teachers, and administration for the opportunity to learn and to share.

Thank you to our Instructional Facilitator Team at Fort Wayne Community. You are awesome!

Thank you to Joanna for her patience and encouragement.

✳ ✳ ✳

Cover Design by Maria Lilja
Cover Illustration by Kristen Balouch
Interior Design by Sarah Morrow

Copyright © 2006 by Kathleen Hurni-Dove
All rights reserved.
Published by Scholastic Inc.
Printed in the U.S.A.
ISBN 0-439-44401-2

6 7 8 9 10 40 11

Table of Contents

Introduction

For the past twenty years, teaching students to write has been a personal journey. As a teacher, I've watched myself transition from story starters to writing formulas, to class bookmaking, until I arrived at writing workshop, which is truly the most powerful approach I've experienced. When I established my first community of writers, I knew a workshop that allowed students the opportunity to create their own authentic writing pieces was the best choice for teaching students to write. Writing workshop provides differentiation. Every young writer works at his or her own pace within the writing cycle. During workshop time, I see drafting, revising, conferring—most importantly, I see writers who care deeply about each other's writing.

As a writing consultant and facilitator, I assist teachers with implementing a workshop format in their classrooms. As a first step, I help teachers create a safe classroom environment where the teacher and students work side by side in a community rich with print, language, and literature. Within this community, we offer students modeling, demonstration, and lots and lots of practice. Next, we teach our students to become a receptive audience for each other. As part of an audience, young writers not only learn to listen and talk like writers, but also they develop a respect for each other's work.

A writing workshop has many advantages; it

- encourages a love of writing
- develops independence and responsibility
- allows students the opportunity to discover their own writing process
- provides students with life-long tools
- teaches students to think and envision possibilities
- differentiates learning
- creates an appreciation and understanding of both craft and genre
- fosters respect for writing and each other

I believe students become better writers when they are provided daily opportunities to write during a workshop. Choice of topic encourages ownership. Studying genre and immersing students with quality literature helps students learn the writing craft. Most importantly, students discover their own process. Through thinking, planning, and practice, they learn how they work as writers. With our encouragement and support in a workshop, young writers will develop a lifelong love of writing.

Chapter 1

Crafting Fiction Leads

On the subject of leads, most writing teachers are in agreement: a good lead should grab the audience. The question of course, is *how* to do that. What is it that makes an opening grab or "hook" the reader? What is it that makes an opening hook you? It's my belief that the best leads use the power of language to make contact with the reader's feelings. Once the reader's feelings have been engaged, we might say the reader is "hooked."

I was hooked by the very first lines of Abby and Sarah Levine's *Sometimes I Wish I Were Mindy*. I was standing in the bookstore, and as soon as I read the first few lines of the book, I knew I wanted to buy it to share with my students. The very first sentence, only five words long, is "My friend Mindy is rich." In fact, Mindy is very rich. She has a big house with multiple bathrooms, fancy furniture, lots of toys, and a swimming pool.

Most children at one time or another wish they were rich. Many long for a backyard swimming pool or other such luxuries. And, like the narrator, most have had the fleeting wish that they were somebody else. The emotion on display here is envy—and it's part of the human experience. The author lets us feel from the very first lines how intensely the narrator is caught in the grip of her emotion. And so, because we are human, we are engaged.

Moon Ball by Jane Yolen is another book I purchased after reading just the first page. In the second sentence we get to the crux of the matter: Danny Brower has just struck out. This wasn't just any strikeout; this was the final strikeout, the one that ends the game. The opposing team erupts into cheers of joy, taunting Danny with names like "hitless wonder." With immediate, poetic language and in just a few swift strokes, Yolen brings us right into the middle of this very real heartache. There's not a young boy or girl who has ever struck out that hasn't experienced the same feelings as Danny in that moment. Nor is there a parent who has watched his child strike out that hasn't felt the same emotional pain as Danny Brower. And Yolen accomplishes all this in just the first few lines! The reader wants to know how Danny handles his adversity. Does he ever gain the confidence he needs to hit the ball? As soon as I read the beginning I was hooked, and I bought the book for my son. Jane Yolen grabbed me on the very first page with a beginning that made an emotional connection with me.

There are many types of leads. As I've suggested, for a beginning to work, it must allow the reader to make a connection. And if the connection is an emotional one (rather than merely intellectual), the beginning will have even more power. Because all readers come to a piece of literature with a multitude of experiences, it is the feeling, the emotion of a well-written beginning that keeps us turning the page. If there isn't a connection tied to either feeling or experience, we are apt to put the book down and choose a different selection.

In her book *What's Your Story?*, Marion Dane Bauer gives young writers the following advice about beginnings:

> *Remember that the most important words of any piece you write are those you open with. They will draw your readers in or turn them away. They will also create a solid base upon which all the rest of the story will stand. . . .*

Types of Fictional Leads

There are probably as many ways to begin a piece of fiction or narrative writing as there are writers. (Please note that my discussion in this section pertains to personal narratives as well as fictional stories, because the techniques of storytelling apply whether the narrative is wholly made up or comes from real life.) The main idea we want to convey to our students is that the beginning's "job" is to hook the reader. To the extent that the lead gets that crucial job done, it works. Still, we can classify most leads into one of eight types, and it's an excellent idea for you and your students to familiarize yourselves with some of these leads in a variety of books. These types of beginnings are easy to find in your school and classroom libraries. Eight common ways to begin a piece of fictional or other narrative writing are:

- begin with a question
- begin with action
- begin with a problem
- begin with the setting
- begin with dialogue
- begin with a sound
- begin with character description
- begin with a thought.

If you pick up most any piece of high-quality children's literature, you are likely to find one of these beginnings. However, below I've listed a few titles that illustrate each type of lead. You might wish to look at these books, for clear illustrations of each type of lead and share the leads with your students. You may want to check other professional resources for additional types of leads to use with various genres. This will assist you in differentiating for those students who are advanced writers. Remember a lead can be a sentence, several sentences, a paragraph, or in a longer work, the first few pages.

✳ **Begin with a question**

Grandma's Smile by Elaine Moore
The Book of Bad Ideas by Laura Huliska-Beith
Hey, Little Ant by Phillip and Hannah Hoose

* **Begin with action**

  Freedom School, Yes! by Amy Littlesugar
  Because of Winn-Dixie by Kate DiCamillo
  Try Again Sally Jane by Mary Diestel-Feddersen

* **Begin with a problem**

  Dear Willie Rudd, Libba Moore Gray
  When Sophie Gets Angry—Really, Really Angry by Molly Bang
  I Was a Second Grade Werewolf by Daniel Pinkwater

* **Begin with the setting**

  Sounder by William H. Armstrong
  Roxaboxen by Alice McLerran
  Ruby Mae Has Something to Say by David Small

* **Begin with dialogue**

  Bea and Mr. Jones by Amy Schwartz
  Frederick's Alligator by Esther Peterson
  The Seashore Book by Charlotte Zolotow

* **Begin with a sound**

  Cook-A-Doodle-Doo! by Susan Stevens Crummel
  The Pigeon Finds a Hot Dog! by Mo Willems
  The Monster Trap by Dean Morrissey

* **Begin with character description**

  Miz Berlin Walks by Jane Yolen
  Sleeping Ugly by Jane Yolen
  Mr. Lincoln's Way by Patricia Polacco

* **Begin with a thought**

  My Mama Had a Dancing Heart by Libba Moore Gray
  The Terrible Thing That Happened At Our House by Marge Blaine
  Little Nino's Pizzeria by Karen Barbour

Strategy: Introduce Students to a Variety of Leads

One of the best ways to get young writers to improve the beginnings of their stories is by sharing powerful leads with them. In preparation for this lesson, gather together books with great beginnings. You may choose some from the list above, but there is no end of stories with winning leads. I find that limiting the number of books is the most difficult part of the preparation for this lesson. Depending on how much time you have, you might use anywhere from three to six books. Try to find titles that illustrate a variety of leads. Also, see if you can find beginnings that hook your students while sparking an emotional connection.

Focus Lesson 1: Sharing Powerful Leads

After you have selected the books, call your students to the classroom meeting area. Tell students that you have been looking through books in search of great beginnings. Starting with one of the books, read the opening sentences (or paragraphs) to the class. Then, after reading the beginning, ask the students if the book is one they would like to keep on reading. Discuss what it is about each beginning that makes them yearn for more. Read just enough to whet their appetites. When you read aloud, do so with expression and passion, modeling for students how others will read their stories. This gives them food for thought. How will their leads sound when others read them aloud? Below is a sample lesson with my second graders.

Mrs. H-D: Writers, have you ever thought about what makes you want to turn the page when you open a book? In other words, how do authors hook their readers?

Steven: Sometimes authors hook you when they begin with something scary like "One dark night, nobody was home." If the author begins like that, I want to keep reading because I know something is going to happen and I want to find out what it is.

Mrs. H-D: Steven, I heard you say that writers hook their readers with something scary. I also heard you give us an example when you used the words "One dark night, nobody was home." That is scary to think about. Using your example, can you tell me how you think the author created that feeling?

Steven: I'm not sure.

Adele: I think I know. If the author wrote "One dark night, nobody was home," then he was kind of doing two things. He was telling us the setting when he said *one dark night*, and he told us what the problem might be when he said *nobody was home*.

Mrs. H-D: Good thinking, Adele. Actually writers may use setting to hook you. When the writing is vivid, we feel like we are right *there*. Or they might use the problem, or they might use a combination of the two.

Brandon: Sometimes writers use questions to hook you.

Mrs. H-D: You're right. Questions are great hooks. They make us want to respond. Now, writers, I'm going to read you several beginnings from a variety of books. I want you to think about whether or not the author's hook keeps you wanting to turn the page. And I also want you to be prepared to tell me how the author hooked you.

The first lead I read is from Audrey Wood's book *The Red Racer*. The character, Nona, is on her way to school when the chain on her bike comes off, the brakes jam, and she goes flying over the handlebars. Worst of all, she falls right in front of a group of kids she refers to as the "brats." Students usually love this beginning. Let's listen in.

Mrs. H-D: Should I turn the page?

Melissa: Yes. I want to know if Nona is hurt and who the brats are.

Mrs. H-D: Melissa, say more about the way the author hooked you.

Melissa: The author used lots of action. She also used strong verbs like *pedaled, jammed,* and *crashed.*

Mrs. H-D: So Melissa, you are saying Audrey Wood makes you want to turn the page when she began her piece with both action and strong verbs that helped you see that action.

Melissa: Yes!

Next I read the beginning of *Shortcut* by Donald Crews. In this opening, the narrator tells us he and his siblings decided to take a shortcut even though he knows they should have taken the road. This story's lead has the students hanging on every word. They can't wait to hear more. The words *shortcut* and *should have* click with students. They connect right away. Children know taking a shortcut means danger.

Listen in on this conversation.

Nathan: Mrs. H-D, please keep turning the pages.

Mrs. H-D: Obviously Donald Crews has you hooked, Nathan. Tell me why.

Nathan: Because I know those kids might be in trouble.

Mrs. H-D: How do you know?

Nathan: Because the author wrote *shortcut* and I took a shortcut once and I got in lots of trouble.

Mrs. H-D: I see. You have a personal connection. Please tell me more about how Donald Crews hooked you.

Nathan: By starting with setting?

Melissa: He also used strong verbs like *listened* and *decided.*

Steven: Donald Crews did the same thing I did when I said, "One dark night, nobody was home." I think he used setting and maybe a little action.

Mrs. H-D: Good thinking, writers!

The last lead I read in this lesson is Kathleen Stevens's *The Beast in the Bathtub.* Writers are sometimes told to "begin in the middle of things." This is excellent advice, and Kathleen Stevens does exactly that. There's no buildup, no establishing of character or setting. From the get-go we are right in the middle of the problem, as Lewis announces that he can't take a bath because there's a beast in the bathtub. As you can see, this lead appeals to students.

Mrs. H-D: Well, what do you think? Do you want me to turn the page?

Justin: I want you to turn the page because I want to find out what's in the bathtub. It can't really be a beast. I think the author uses humor.

Mrs. H-D: Say more about how the author uses humor.

Justin: When the little kid yells *he can't take a bath because of the beast in the tub,* it's silly and funny.

Adele: Another thing is, the author uses dialogue in the beginning to hook the reader.

Mrs. H-D: Good point.

When you finish reading the different beginnings, put the books in a place where they're easily accessible to students. If they haven't heard or read these titles, they will want to read them as soon as possible. Next, take students to the school library. Give them fifteen to twenty minutes to look for three books with a great beginning. After the students select their books, have them gather in small groups and share their books with classmates. Students enjoy this activity. It allows them the opportunity to take a deeper look at how authors begin their stories. It also teaches them to turn to literature when they are having difficulty writing a beginning. In addition, it provides you with the chance to view titles with which you may not be familiar.

An excellent follow-up activity is to have students make a display of leads. Give each student several note cards and send them back to the library. This time ask students to find three lead sentences that hook the reader. Instruct them to write the hooks on their note cards. Then ask students how they would classify the hook. Let them think for a while. How did the author draw the reader in? Through their own exploration, students will discover that literary elements like dialogue, questions, and setting are excellent choices for good leads. After student discussion, display the cards with the leads the students found. The display can be used as a quick reference. If your students keep a writer's notebook, you may ask them to tab and label a section for leads. Then when they come across a lead they like, they can write it in their notebook. Later, these leads can serve as references when they need to craft a beginning of their own.

Sample of Student Work

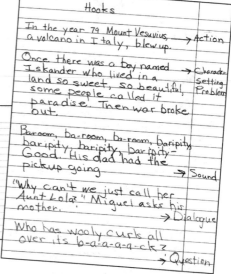

Strategy: Encourage Students to Return to Their Own Writing and Rewrite Leads

When I teach writing, I rely on daily anecdotal notes. During my planning time, I review the notes and I look for patterns. As teachers of writing, we need to base our instruction on student need. For instance, when I conference with students, I notice certain trends among their leads. Most of them begin generically. I'm sure you've encountered the following:

- Hi, my name is—

- Once upon a time . . .
- My story is about my cat, Snickers.

It doesn't matter whether you work with second, third, or fourth graders. They all rally around those bland beginnings. You may wish to address this individually, with a small group of students, or with the entire class—although in order to really get young writers crafting strong beginnings, repeated instruction in all of these settings will yield rich rewards.

Focus Lesson 2: Rewrite a Lead

For this lesson I choose five different types of leads and select books with examples of each. I read each lead aloud and briefly discuss the strategy the author used in his or her writing. On a piece of chart paper, I make five columns and write the different types of leads at the top: Question, Action, Dialogue, and so on. Then I encourage students to give one of the beginnings a try in their own writing. Some students will draft a new piece. Others will find a piece they've already written and try rewriting their beginning a couple of times using various leads. The activity works well in either situation.

I give students some time to work on their beginnings. Then I ask them to write their name on the chart underneath the type of lead they tried. When it's sharing time, students don't share their whole piece; they share only their new beginning. Because most writers want to share, this activity encourages students to try different leads.

Sample of Student Work

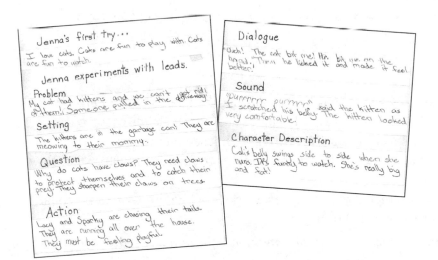

Leads

A Question

Dialogue

Setting

Sound

Action

Character Description

A Thought

A Problem

Strategy: Model Rewriting Leads in Several Ways

Most school districts require students to respond to at least three writing prompts during the school year. Even though prompts are not authentic assessments, they provide students with practice and teachers with useful information about students' readiness to respond in writing during a test situation. Whenever I read a large number of writing-prompt responses from several classrooms, one fact consistently jumps out at me: most students lack the ability to write effective beginnings. One of the reasons beginnings pose problems for young writers is that students assume the audience is aware of who and what they are writing about. But perhaps the most common explanation for lackluster beginnings is that students simply don't know how else to begin. Note that in the following lesson, the prompt asks students to write a personal, or true, narrative from their own experience. As mentioned earlier, I'm including personal narratives here in the discussion of fictional beginnings because the storytelling techniques share much in common.

Focus Lesson 3: Modeling Leads With Your Own Writing

To come at beginnings from a different direction, I use a focus lesson. First I read the book *Some Things are Scary* by Florence Parry Heide. Then I ask students to address the following prompt:

> *At one time or another we are all afraid of something. Write a story about a time when you were scared. Make sure your story has a beginning, middle, and end. The beginning should capture the attention of the audience.*

Unless we've already done a lot of work on leads—and sometimes even when we have—students will invariably write leads like these:

- Hi my name is _____!
- I was scared when I was at a park because there was a big guy coming towards me.
- A kid scared me.
- I was scared.

I listen to students as they share their leads, and then I explain that in a little while, they're going to rewrite their leads. But first I want to share some leads of my own.

Next I share some sample leads that I've written. I choose an entirely different subject, since the goal for a lesson like this is for students to flexibly transfer what they learn to their own writing.

I explain to students that recently at a writers' workshop I had to write a personal narrative in response to the following prompt:

> *Write a story about someone who has made a difference in your life.*

On the overhead, I wrote two different lead sentences.

- Hi! My name is Kathy.
- My grandmother made a difference in my life.

Mrs. H-D: Writers, I want you to tell me which of these two sentences is the better lead.

Emma: I think the second one is better than the first.

Mrs. H-D: Please tell us why.

Emma: The second sentence seems like you're focused. I mean, you're staying on topic.

Brad: But it's boring.

Mrs. H-D: I thought I was addressing the topic in the lead sentence.

Spencer: At least it is better than "Hi! My name is Kathy."

Gary: That's the way I start my writing.

Mrs. H-D: Please tell us why you start that way, Gary.

Gary: Because I can't think of anything else, and I want the audience to know who I am.

Brandon: Mrs. H-Dove, why don't you begin with a setting, or action? You've taught us about different beginnings.

Mrs. H-D: That's a great idea. The second lead might be a little better than the first, but it still doesn't grab the reader. On the recent prompt you were just given, I noticed exactly the same kinds of beginnings as the two I put on the overhead.

Next I put the following leads on the overhead for the students to read. Usually I omit the type of lead, and let students determine for themselves.

- *The sheets on the bed smelled crisp and clean. Grandma washed and ironed them daily. There were two twin beds in the room. One for grandma. One for me. I heard the bathwater draining. I watched the moon while waiting for a night-time story.* (Setting)

- *Oo oo-oo-oo-OO-OO! The teakettle whistled. I knew it was time for lunch. Grandmother drank hot tea with every meal.* (Sound)

- *"Get your jacket. We're going on a roller coaster ride!" I couldn't believe it. Grandma convinced Grandpa to take us to Crystal Beach.* (Dialogue)

- *Grandma swung at the snake with her hoe. Over and over she thumped the ground as the snake slowly retreated.* (Action)

- *Grandmother's hair was white and wispy. Her skin was soft and wrinkly. Her knuckles swollen. My dad said her bony knuckles were the result of arthritis.* (Character Description)

- *If you could spend the day with anyone in the world, who would you choose? I would choose my Grandmother Kate.* (Question)

- *Grandmother Kate made my childhood not only special, but also exciting.* (Thought)

As I display each beginning, I ask the students to identify the type of lead I used. Of course, different students will have their favorites. The lead using action fascinates Sean. He wants to know the whole story. McKenzie loves roller coasters. Immediately she makes a personal connection. The character description sparks an emotional connection with Daniel because his mother has rheumatoid arthritis. The students agree that all of these endings grab them far more than the two lackluster leads we looked at earlier. They get the point.

Now I ask them to try revising the beginnings of their stories about the time they were scared. The focus is on rewriting their beginnings only. Remind students to concentrate on only one area of improvement. Otherwise they will become overwhelmed and discouraged.

(Of course, when students revise their leads, they sometimes wish to revise other parts too, but that's not the point of this activity.) The following are revised beginnings.

Samples of Student Work

The Nightmare Horror!!!!!!!!

This wasn't any ordinary dream. You could feel what was happening to you!
Well, you see I was just walking I see a gray blob in the air and squinted my eyes.
My goodness! It was jaws floating in the air! Oh no! He spotted me. I saw a door!
I ran! It came to close and bit my arm off! It hurt so bad! I ran towards the door!
I was so weak that I landed on a soft surface. The door was steel! Jaws couldn't
get through. We went up and got the cats. I got Fritsee. He looked at me! And
guess what! His eyes turned lava red! I dropped him. He jumped up and bit me!

The Spider

Once there was a spider happily spinning a web that looked like silky lace
and felt as soft as cotton balls. The spider was very pleased with himself.

Strategy: Teach Students to Evaluate Leads Using Criteria Charts

We want our students to be able to zero in on the qualities that make writing excellent. These qualities are not unique to beginnings, but by focusing on them, we can help students to consider what makes strong writing sing. The more we do this, the more we help them bring strong writing to their beginnings, as well as their middles and endings.

Focus Lesson 4: Using a Criteria Chart to Explore Strong Leads

For this lesson, you'll want to choose a piece of literature that's appropriate for your students. Second graders will need a simple piece, whereas fourth graders, who have been exposed to a lot of writing, will be ready for something more sophisticated. However, if fourth graders have been in classrooms where a writing workshop hasn't been a part of the curriculum, you'll have a lot more work to do as far as introducing and modeling the qualities of a well-written piece of writing.

I encourage you to look through books and find a piece with not only an interesting beginning but also with strong vocabulary, fluency, organization, and elaboration. Once you find a suitable piece, retype the text and make an overhead transparency. With a group of fourth graders, I use Deborah Hopkinson's *Bluebird Summer*. Hopkinson uses vivid language to set the scene.

I start the lesson by having the students read and reflect on the beginning. I ask them to take a deep look at the writing by carefully thinking about the literary techniques the author used to help make this a strong beginning. As students respond to *Blueberry Summer*, I make a criteria chart. I take a large sheet of chart paper and label it "High-Quality Leads." When students identify writing techniques that make a high-quality beginning, I list them on the chart. Let's listen in.

Mrs. H-D: Who can tell me what kind of story beginning Deborah Hopkinson used?

Ann: She used setting.

Mrs. H-D: How do you know?

Ann: Okay. She's talking about the farm and wheat fields. She also says something about dust and plowing and a barn.

Mrs. H-D: She does mention all those things. Her words paint the setting for the reader. How does she do that?

Brandon: She describes the wheat fields with the simile *like a golden sea.*

Damian: I like when she used the verb *washes.*

Mrs. H-D: What are some other things she has effectively done as a writer to make this a strong beginning?

Ricky: She doesn't use the same word to start her sentences. Every sentence begins with a different word.

Lisa: This author appealed to my sense of taste.

Mrs. H-D: What do you mean?

Lisa: When she says *the hot taste of dust in his mouth*, it just made my throat feel dry. I like those words. I wish they were mine.

Mrs. H-D: Writers, I've heard you mention strong verbs, simile, varied sentence beginnings, and appealing to the senses. I'm pleased with the way you are becoming familiar with the traits of quality writing. In order for a writer to craft a strong beginning, or for that matter any piece of writing, the writer needs to be familiar with and study good literature. Today, I'd like all of you to select a piece of writing from your writing folder and try to polish the beginning with some of the same literary elements you discovered in *Bluebird Summer.* Please refer to the High-Quality Beginnings Criteria Chart as you polish your work. Can you substitute stronger verbs? Can you bring in a simile? Have you appealed to the senses? Are your sentences varied in length?

> ### Quality Leads Criteria Chart
>
> - Paints setting for reader
> - Uses simile
> - Includes strong verbs
> - Varies sentence beginnings
> - Appeals to the senses

I've been teaching the writing process for almost twenty years. Apart from consistently providing students with time to write, I believe that exposing them to the elements of high-quality writing through the use of excellent literature is the single best way to help them become strong writers. What's more, students will not only become better writers, they will become better readers.

Sample of Student Work

Dance

Tap! Tap! Tap! (We are in the Ballroom)

It's the most wonderfulest place to be. You get to twirl, swirl, and of course dance! Its peaceful and fun. Also if you compete you'll win cool prizes like a medaliane, trophie, and new costumes! You even might win and go to the next state like Tennessee or Ohio or maybe even New York! I like dancing, and maybe you will to if you practice, Dance, practice and try it out. By. Kileena H., 8 years old

In this chapter we explored ways to help students craft beginnings for fictional writing. In the next chapter, we examine strategies for writing beginnings to nonfiction writing.

Chapter 1 Review

- Introduce students to various types of beginnings fiction writers use.
- Share models of strong leads from literature.
- Encourage student to rewrite their beginnings once they've finished a piece.
- Model writing several leads for the same piece.

Chapter 2

Crafting Nonfiction Leads

When I was a young, I loved to keep journals. I included many entries that consisted of personal experiences, stories I created, and artifacts. More than anything, my journals resembled a writer's notebook. I craved this kind of writing mostly because I did not have the opportunity to write that way in school. Most of the writing I did in school was the formulaic type. You know the kind: make sure you have a topic sentence, supporting details, and conclusion. I despised writing book reports, informational reports, and newspaper articles. Even worse, I didn't know great writing consisted of such things as voice, fluency, sense of audience, and strong vocabulary. Nobody ever told me that strong verbs are critical when writing a report or an article. Even though teachers talked about style, I didn't really understand which literary elements created style.

Today in schools, writing takes on many different forms. Young students write many narrative pieces whether they are fiction or nonfiction. In addition, state standards require second, third, and fourth grade students to write letters, persuasive pieces, and literary response. Most state testing consists of nonfiction. The bottom line is that students need to be reading and writing more nonfiction than ever.

As I mentioned earlier, I used to despise writing reports because they felt boring and lifeless, devoid of any personality or spark. Now, I understand that nonfiction writing can be as rich and evocative as fiction. More and more teachers are finding ways to teach students to write nonfiction the way *real* writers do it, making the process as enjoyable for students as the personal and fictional narratives many of them love to write. As teachers of writing, we must show students how to examine nonfiction as closely as fiction. Students can learn to write great nonfiction by studying books, magazines, and newspaper articles. What's more, students can learn how to write nonfiction beginnings that capture the interest of the audience by examining well-written nonfiction.

We can let our students know that the idea that nonfiction writing is meant only to inform is inaccurate. Whether students are reading nonfiction or writing it, they should know that nonfiction writing can entertain and engage the reader every bit as much as fiction writing. Strong writing is strong writing, no matter what the genre.

The following strategies, focus lessons, and examples of student work demonstrate the methods I've used with students to encourage them to write effective nonfiction beginnings.

Strategy: Familiarize Students With a Variety of Nonfiction Leads

As is the case with fiction, exposure to a variety of nonfiction leads will get your students thinking about new ways to begin their nonfiction, informational writing.

Focus Lesson 1: Two-Column Notes

In this lesson, students will record nonfiction beginnings and their responses to them. You may wish to use this as a shared writing lesson with a large group. Or, you may give students their own two-column note paper, or have them record this activity in their writing notebook.

Following is a sample lesson.

Mrs. H-D: Today we are going to look through nonfiction books to see how the writers of those pieces kept your interest. If you look at the chart paper, you will see I have drawn two columns. I labeled the first column "Beginning" and the second column "My Response." Notice under the Beginning column, I've written a sample of a beginning from a book written by Jim Arnosky called *All About Sharks*. Let's read this beginning together.

> *Have you ever wondered about sharks?*
> *How big do they grow?*
> *How sharp are their teeth?*
> *What do they eat?*
> *Why do they attack people?*
>
> *This book answers all of these questions and more.*
> *It's all about sharks!*

After reading the beginning together, I ask students to respond with their thoughts and I record their responses in the appropriate column.

Mrs. H-D: Would someone like to share their thoughts concerning Arnosky's beginning?

Sam: He starts with a question.

Rick: He starts with a lot of questions. I haven't noticed many writers do that before.

Mrs. H-D: Rick, why do you think he used a lot of questions?

Rick: Say you want to write your own piece about sharks. If I read his beginning, I would know some of the information that is in the book.

I would know it would be a good book for me to read and take notes on. I like the way he asks the reader five questions and then he tells us more questions will be answered about sharks. I would read this book because I'm sure I'll find the answers. I'd like to try this kind of beginning with the biography I'm writing.

Now, in the Response column, I write Rick's response, namely that he likes all the questions at the beginning because they let him know that the author is going to answer to all these questions and more.

Picking up on Rick's point, I point out to students that what the author is doing in the beginning of this book is *making a promise to the reader*. He's telling readers what they are going to learn by reading his book. Making such a promise is another excellent way for writers to begin a piece of nonfiction writing. A promise at the beginning lets the reader know what to expect. It also reminds the writer of the path he or she is on. A promise at the beginning can help with revision as well. Students can ask themselves if they've kept their promise. If not, they can see what they need to add in order to do so.

Mrs. H-D: Writers, I'm going to give you the next twenty minutes to explore the nonfiction section of our classroom library. Using your two-column charts, record several nonfiction beginnings. Then record your response to the beginning. Think about the following things: Does the lead hook you? What kind of lead did the writer choose? Name it. Why do you think the author chose the lead? Does the lead show and not tell? Is the lead clear and concise? Does the author make a promise in the beginning that lets you know what lies ahead?

Sample of Student Work

It was the night of The Wishing Sky and Amelia was spending the night with her grandma, Noanie.
"Our star cookies smell so good!" Amelia watched as Noanie pulled the tray of cookies from the oven.

My Response
Why I liked it
Because I'm wondering about the Wishing Sky and what that means.

Once upon a time way out in the desert, there were three little javelinas. Javelinas (ha-ve-LEE-nas) are wild, hairy, southwestern cousins of pigs.
Their heads were hairy, their backs were hairy, and their bony legs—all the way down to their hard little hooves—were very hairy. But their snouts were soft and pink.

This beginning makes me think of pigs in cowboy boots.

Strategy: Help Students Notice Nonfiction Leads in Multiple Sources

I want my students to know that nonfiction writing surrounds them, not just in the classroom but out in the "real world" as well. And just as fiction writing must hook the reader, so too must nonfiction. Nowhere is this more true than in newspaper articles. A story's headline is its first attempt to grab the reader. Then, the article itself must follow through.

Focus Lesson 2: What Hooks You at Home?

I present this lesson to the whole class, and then I assign independent research as homework.

Mrs. H-D: Writers, last night as I was reading the evening newspaper, I was thinking about leads. I went through the newspaper and marked all the beginnings that hooked me. I'd like to share a few of these with you. As I share, I'd like you to think about why these beginnings hooked me. What was the writer doing?

The weather wasn't the only thing that was hot in Hamilton on Tuesday morning, apparently so was the car [name] of Stockton, Calif., was driving. To remedy the situation [name] drove his vehicle into the water near the beach.

Mrs. H-D: Who would like to respond?

Mandy: I can't believe it. Why would anyone drive their car into water?

Mrs. H-D: Mandy, why do you think this beginning hooked me? Once I started reading, I couldn't put the paper down. I had to read the entire article.

Mandy: I think you were hooked because the author began with action.

Mrs. H-D: Tell us more.

Mandy: Well, the article might have started like this—a man from Stockton, California, drove his car into the water. That would have been boring. I guess it's the way the writer wrote it. He compared the outside temperature and the car temperature and he got right to the point about what the man did to solve the problem.

Mrs. H-D: Mandy, you asked us an important question. Why would anyone drive their car into water? Do you think this beginning hooked you enough to keep you reading?

Mandy: Yes! I want to know why he did it. Was it an accident, or was it on purpose?

Mrs. H-D: Let's listen to the next one.

> *A spadefood toad sits and waits. The toad has been in its burrow under the desert sand for many months. It is not exactly asleep. It is not exactly hibernating. It is just waiting.*
>
> *The toad lives in a desert area called the Great Basin. Hardly any rain falls there. Sand and rocks spread for miles and miles. There are no shady places where a toad can hide from the blazing summer sun.*

What do you think?

Carrie: The writer started with the setting.

Billy: The writer was showing, not telling.

Devin: The writer left me wondering about what the toad is waiting for. I know a toad will die if it doesn't keep cool.

Mrs. H-D: Great. Let's try one more.

> *Is a pot-bellied pig considered livestock or a pet? Can a dog ever be considered a cat? Why did the chicken cross the road in Auburn? Why did the alligator cross the road in Kendallville?*

Are you hooked?

Sarah: Two things hooked me. The article begins with a series of questions like some of Jim Arnosky's books. And I want to know the answer to the questions, especially the one about the alligator crossing the road in Kendallville. Alligators don't walk across the streets if you live in the north.

Mrs. H-D: Yes. That's why I was hooked. My curiosity piqued with the last question. I wondered the same thing. I felt some concern that such an exotic animal may be on the loose. I wanted to read further. Will anyone share what you learned from our discussion about beginnings I found in the evening newspaper?

Daniel: I learned reading a newspaper might be interesting.

Megan: I learned writers of newspaper articles need to hook their readers.

Mrs. H-D: Nonfiction writing takes on many forms. This is what I'd like you to do. This evening, browse through newspapers, magazines, or even mail such as brochures, letters, and advertisements. Find beginnings that hook you. Cut them out and bring them to workshop tomorrow morning. Be prepared to share and discuss the beginnings that really hooked you, and tell us why.

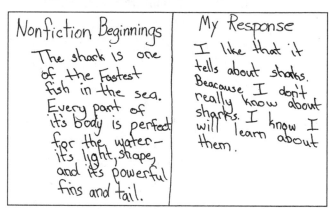

Nonfiction Beginnings
The shark is one of the fastest fish in the sea. Every part of it's body is perfect for the water— it's light, shape, and it's powerful fins and tail.

My Response
I like that it tells about sharks. Beacause I don't really know about sharks. I know I will learn about them.

Strategy: Teach Students to Analyze Multiple Leads on the Same Topic

Our students have access to a wealth of information. For example, think of a famous person that your students may wish to research, such as Abraham Lincoln. Information about Abraham Lincoln can be found in a variety of picture books written from various points of view, as well as poetry, periodicals, encyclopedias, and on various Web sites.

Once students analyze several types of leads written for pieces on the same topic, they are very likely to try out different kinds in their own writing.

Focus Lesson 3: How Do Different Authors Approach the Same Topic?

While working with a fourth-grade class on biographies, I presented the following lesson on beginnings. I wanted the students to understand how several authors approached their writing from different perspectives and thus their beginnings would be different. I chose the following titles: *Home Run* by Robert Burleigh, *The Babe and I* by David Adler, and *Babe Ruth* by Guernsey Van Riper, Jr. Then I typed up the beginnings of each book and made overhead transparencies.

The three beginnings I've chosen for this lesson are leads that contain a promise, a scene, and action. You can choose any three leads to illustrate the idea that a single topic can be approached in a variety of ways.

The students and I read the beginnings as part of a shared reading activity. Please listen in on the following discussion.

Mrs. H-D: Writers, let's discuss each of these pieces of writing about Babe Ruth. Let's look at *Home Run* first. What did you notice about this beginning?

Adam: I noticed the author is telling about Babe Ruth from outside the story.

Mrs. H-D: Yes, it is written in third person.

Josepha: He writes with passion when he tells about how much Babe loves the game.

Tia:	The author makes you a promise. You know you will find out how Babe Ruth changes the game forever.
Mrs. H-D:	This is a simple beginning that is clear, concise, and meaningful. The author really sets an informative, but gentle tone for the story. Now let's look at David Adler's *The Babe and I*. The approach to the topic is completely different. This is a work of fiction, but some of the events about Babe Ruth's life like the home runs, collapse, visit with the fans in Yankee Stadium, and pinch-hitting experiences are all based on events that actually happened. What did you notice about the beginning?
Max:	I noticed that the author started this piece with a scene.
Mrs. H-D:	Say more. For instance, tell us what the scene teaches you.
Max:	It taught me that back in 1932 many people were poor. Lots of people didn't have jobs. That this story took place during the Great Depression. The character in the story thinks he is lucky.
Mrs. H-D:	I hear you saying that beginning with a well-written scene sets the mood for the writing. Does anyone else have something to add?
Adele:	This book makes me see that you can learn true things by mixing them in a fiction story. And you can use some of the same story beginnings with fiction and nonfiction.
Mrs. H-D:	Exactly. Great thinking. Now let's take a look now at Guernsey Van Riper, Jr.'s, beginning.
Sam:	That one is my favorite. It begins with lots of action. The reader also learns about Babe Ruth.
Mrs. H-D:	Tell us a little about what you learned, Sam.
Sam:	I learned he got into lots of trouble, but he really didn't mean to. And his mom and dad really didn't pay much attention to him. And his mom was sick. Oh, and he didn't go to school. Could I please borrow that book?
Mrs. H-D:	Sure Sam.

Mrs. H-D: Writers, this morning we have looked at the way three different authors approached the same topic—by making a promise, by showing a scene, and by jumping into action. All three had different ideas about how to hook you so you'd keep reading about the life of Babe Ruth. Now, I'd like you to return to your own biographies. Carefully read your beginnings. Try to approach your beginning using one of these three strategies. Use either a simple beginning with a promise, a scene, or a beginning full of action.

Sample of Student Work

Did you know Anne Frank and her family wore yellow stars on their clothing?
Did you know her family wasn't allowed to go to parks, or ride in cars or trains?

And did you know Anne Frank and her family hid in an apartment with other Jewish people?

This story answers all these questions and much more. On the following pages you will learn all about Anne Frank.

Anne Frank listened to the bombs explode, the gunfire crackle, and sirens wail. She wondered how long she and her family would be safe.

Strategy: Use Quickwrites to Generate Multiple Leads

One of the great benefits of quickwrites is that because of their time pressure, writers tend to dispense with self-censoring. When the clock is ticking madly, there's simply no time for self-censorship! Students just have to get something, anything, down on the page. I have found that some of my students' richest work is begun in a quickwrite session.

In the following lesson, students brainstorm not one, but three leads to a piece of writing. I like the idea of generating multiple leads. When students have a chance to create several leads, they are freed up to experiment and take risks. If the experiment doesn't work, it's perfectly okay because they have other possibilities.

Focus Lesson 4: Quickwrite Leads

In this lesson, students write three leads to a piece that they're writing on an area of expertise. I begin the lesson by asking students to make a list of all the things they are an expert at. All of us are experts at something. I ask students what they do well so they could teach others about it. (For instance, I consider myself an expert at running, grand-parenting, and procrastinating. Those three areas I could teach others about.)

I allow three minutes for them to generate a list, telling them that they may return to the list at another time.

After students generate their list, together we make a list of all the different ways they might write a good lead.

Next, I ask students to circle, star, or check the one area of expertise they would most like to write about. After students select one area of expertise, I ask them to look at the Lead Chart and choose one of the leads to begin with. Then I set the timer for three minutes, and students write their first lead. When they've finished, we do it twice more. Each time, students select a different type of lead and use it to begin their piece about the same area of expertise.

Let's listen in to Sydney's leads. Her area of expertise is living with an older brother.

Leads

1. Begin with a question
2. Begin with a series of questions
3. Begin with dialogue
4. Begin with sound
5. Begin with surprise
6. Begin with action
7. Begin with setting
8. Begin with promise
9. Begin with problem

Sydney: I chose a question, a surprise, and dialogue for my leads. My first one is a series of questions.

First quickwrite:

Do you ever get annoyed?
Do you ever feel frustrated?
Have you ever wanted to yell so loud glass breaks?
Do you have an older brother?
Well I do, and he is so mean. That is until the day I got sick.

This is my second quickwrite. I used a surprise lead.

Ten Ways to Survive Living With a Big Brother
Never eat Snickers bars that are lying on his desk in his room.
Always cry when he says something mean. (He'll get in trouble.)
Don't listen in on his telephone conversations. (You'll get in trouble.)
If you find money in the pockets of his jeans, don't take it out.
Never, never read the notes you find in his book bag.

That's all I got done.

For the last quickwrite, I used dialogue.

"Forrest, you are in big trouble!"

"Sydney, you are in bigger trouble!"

Do you have a big brother? Well I do and I'm an expert at living with a brother. I want to give you some advice on how to get along with a big brother.

The ability to write compelling leads comes about in two ways. First, students must study effective leads in the texts they encounter, in everything from storybooks to newspaper articles. And second, students must practice writing them. When these two strategies are combined, more and more, students will begin to write leads with flair and feeling.

Chapter 2 Review

- Introduce students to a variety of nonfiction beginnings.
- Explore leads in newspaper and magazine articles.
- Write different kinds of leads for the same topic.
- Encourage students to do quickwrites to generate leads.

Chapter 3

Crafting Fiction Endings

Whether a piece is fiction or nonfiction, the ending is important. The ending is literally the last word, and as such, seems to bear extra weight. In this chapter we'll look at how to help our students bring their fiction and nonfiction pieces to a satisfactory close.

I believe the emotion and feeling that captures the attention of the reader in the beginning can also bring the writing to a close. Endings can bring closure in a number of ways. An ending provide answers. Answers may be predictable, or they may be written with a twist. A twist is a surprise but also gives the reader an unexpected feeling of "yes!" Young writers easily recognize a story with a twist, but it is much more difficult for them to write one. But whether the ending ends with a twist or not, whether it answers questions or poses a few of its own, what's most important is that it leaves the reader feeling satisfied.

Do writers know how their pieces will end before they start writing? Some do and some don't. For many, the writing process is itself one of thinking and discovery. Many writers find that their initial plans are jettisoned once they begin to write and see other possibilities, and others may not have much idea at all where they're going. They just put one foot in front of the other, and trust that they'll find their way.

When teaching beginning writers, however, I find it's helpful if they know where they're headed before they set out. And most young writers feel comforted by having a clear idea of the trail in front of them and where they'll end up. The map for a story or report can be created during prewriting sessions. But even when students know how their pieces will end, they may not know how to write a satisfactory ending.

Endings are not only difficult to write, but also difficult to teach. Students, especially younger students, struggle with the concept of leading the reader to closure. An ending for students of this age is often abrupt. They run out of paper, and therefore the piece has ended. Or maybe they get tired of writing, and so the piece must be finished. The classic ending, which you're no doubt familiar with, is the sudden appendage of the words *The End* in big, bold letters at the end of the page. Other students have such a hard time ending that their pieces go on and on and on. In effect, they don't end. Some students will bring in a culminating event out of nowhere, in which suddenly, the main character is dead. And others will resort to the uninspired "happily ever after." These various difficulties are simply a testament to the challenge young writers, and even not-so-young writers, face in crafting a satisfying ending. In this chapter, we'll look at some ways we can help our students draft a well-written, appropriate ending.

Once you begin to pay close attention to endings, you'll see writers end their stories in a variety of ways, but you'll also discover some trends. You'll notice stories that end with a surprise, a return to the beginning (circular ending), a thought, a feeling, or a memory.

You can use the same kinds of focus lessons to show students how to write effective endings that you used to teach great beginnings. Here is a quick recap of those lessons.

- Collect books with a variety of endings. Share with students.

- Send students to the library to find endings to share with the class. Have students name or identify the ending. Do this individually or in groups.

- Ask students to identify effective endings. Make a chart with their responses.

- When students craft a particular type of ending, have them sign their name under the corresponding column of the Effective Ending Chart. Have students share their endings.

- Students tab a section in their writer's notebook and label endings. Whenever they come across an effective ending, it is added to their notebook.

- Students post titles of books and authors on a leads and endings board. The posting includes the title of book, author, and the type of ending.

> ### Endings
> 1. Circular Ending
> 2. Surprise Ending
> 3. End with a thought
> 4. End with a feeling
> 5. End with a memory

Keep in mind that this book is designed to give you tools for teaching beginnings and endings. A variety of styles and literature examples are provided, but please remember, these are just examples. Each of us needs to create a personal toolbox to share with our students. The books, poems, articles, and samples of writing that will meet the needs of your classroom writing community should be in that box. Use these chapters as a reference to guide you when assembling your own toolbox. Collecting beginnings and endings is fun. Make sure to have some type of filing system in place to keep the great tools you come across.

Writing Endings to Fictional Stories

As with beginnings, there are many ways to end a story. And just as the job of a lead is to hook the reader, the job of the ending is to leave the reader feeling satisfied. The ending should offer a feeling of completeness.

As noted above, to introduce and familiarize your students with different types of endings, you can use some of the same lessons you used for beginnings. The most fruitful way to work on endings is by studying the way professional authors end their pieces. Select a group of books with different endings. For instance, introduce the circular ending with a text such as *If You Give a Pig a Pancake* by Laura Numeroff.

In her book *Wondrous Words* Katie Wood Ray says that:

> *Circular texts have beginnings and endings that match. Typically, many of the same words are used to make this match with some small change to the ending that shows that the text has progressed.*

Using this definition, let's look at the beginning and ending sentences of Laura Numeroff's book.

Beginning: *If you give a pig a pancake, she'll want some syrup to go with it.*

Ending: *And chances are, if she asks you for some syrup, she'll want a pancake to go with it.*

As you can see, Numeroff has circled back and ended up more or less where she began. Other books to share with your students that have this circular pattern are *The Relatives Came* by Cynthia Rylant, *The Stolen Egg* by Sue Vyner, and *The Goodnight Circle* by Carolyn Lesser.

Another type of ending to introduce to your students is the surprise ending, or what I like to call the "twist." It takes skill to write an ending like this. When the story ends, the writer doesn't want to shock the reader. Instead he wants the reader to think, "Oh yes, I should have seen this coming." My favorite text to use for this ending is *The Paperbag Princess* by Robert Munsch. Without spoiling the twist, Munsch prepares the reader by increasing the tension between the two main characters. Although students predict the prince and princess will marry and live happily ever after, the twist makes perfect sense. Everyone is surprised, but in a pleasing way.

As you discuss surprise endings, be sure to make clear to your students that in an ending of this kind, the writer has laid the groundwork for the ending all along. That is to say, a twist is not simply throwing in just any old surprise at the end. Those "out of the blue" surprise endings, in which the main character suddenly dies, for instance, are not satisfying because they aren't grounded in the elements of the story. This is what makes twists so tricky to write.

Try presenting a lesson on twists and then challenge students to write a story with a surprise ending. No matter how "successful" their end result is, they'll have fun attempting to write a story that ends this way.

Many stories, as well as personal narratives, end with a thought, a feeling, or a memory. Helen Ketteman's *I Remember Papa* is a story about a special father-and-son relationship. The author ends with a memory that is poignant, tender, and informative.

For many Saturdays afterward, instead of taking a quarter, I had Papa help me subtract it from my balance, until I had repaid him. Papa's been gone for some years now, but I still have the glove, and I remember.

Here, Ketteman is actually using memory, thought, *and* feeling, all wrapped up in a lovely ending. It's enough to ask our students for one of these, but often, a memory or thought will have a feeling bound up in it. Ideally, this will stay with the reader too.

Strategy: Teach Students How to Write an Effective Ending for a Fictional Story

A fictional narrative needs to have characters, setting, plot, events, and a solution. The ending requires the writer to solve the plot and at the same time, leave the reader feeling satisfied.

Young writers struggle with ending fiction. As noted earlier, this is where students often begin rambling, losing their focus, and slapping down the words *The End*. There are several ways to help students craft solutions. One is by helping them to understand the structure of a fiction story. Another is to teach them some basic plots that are found in fiction. If students understand, for instance, the importance of the having the main character solve his or her own problem, then it becomes easier for them to create an effective solution. If students understand their story should begin close to the end, then they will stay focused on the problem, and stories will arrive more smoothly at a solution.

> Students love the CSP format. It serves two purposes. First it helps them understand story structure. Second, it gives them additional story ideas.

Focus Lesson 1: CSP Character/Setting/Problem

This focus lesson takes place over two days.

Day 1

I begin the lesson by asking students to take out their writers' notebook. Next, I have them insert a tab and label it CSP. C stands for character, S is for setting, and P is for problem. On a large chart, I write CSP several times. Then as a class we complete the CSP on the chart.

Mrs. H-D: Writers, I've noticed that many of you are having difficulty writing an ending to your fiction pieces. For the next couple of days, we are going to look at the important story elements of a fictional story. Understanding the structure of the story will help you know how and when to end your story. First, let's begin by coming up with character. Who will name a character?

Ryan: A boy.

Mrs. H-D: Who will give me a setting?

Ellie: The playground.

Mrs. H-D: Now we need a problem.

Nick: Someone is making fun of him.

Mrs. H-D: Ok, great. Let's try another one. I need another character.

Harold: A puppy.

Mrs. H-D: Now a setting.

Tiarra: A neighborhood.

Mrs. H-D: Now a problem.

Karley: The puppy is lost.

Mrs. H-D: Let's do one more. Who has a character?

Mariah: A grandpa and grandma.

Mrs. H-D: A setting.

> CSPs are great to use during transition times. When students are standing in line or waiting to move on to the next activity, use this as an oral language activity. Simply say, "Give me a character. Give me a setting. Give me a problem. Give me a solution." You might have third and fourth graders take it one step further by suggesting three attempts to solve the problem before arriving at the ultimate solution.

Justin:	A farmhouse.
Mrs. H-D:	Now a problem.
Keith:	The house catches on fire.
Mrs. H-D:	Writers, I'd like you to have a try writing your own CSPs. I am setting the timer for five minutes. Try writing as many as you can. When the timer rings, we will share.

During the five minutes, I write CSPs in my own writer's notebook. I also share my responses. When you write along with your students, you show them you value the writing activity.

C — mailman
S — a quiet neighborhood
P — doesn't deliver mail

C — Miss Candy Sweet
S — works in a candy shop
P — can't eat sweets

C — elephant
S — at the zoo
P — loves to dance, everyone watches her

C — Mr. and Mrs. Cranberry
S — little town grocery
P — their money comes up missing

C — a raccoon and Sarah
S — a campground
P — Sarah's birthday cake is missing

Another great CSP activity is to put Students in groups of four or seven. Place differently colored dots (commercially made) on the back of each student's hand. Each color represents a different part of the story structure—for example:

- Red dot—Character
- Green dot—Setting
- Blue dot—Problem
- Orange dots—Three Events (optional, for older students)
- Yellow dot—Solution

Now, based on what color dot they have, students in each group must come up with the appropriate story element.

Day 2

To start the day's lesson I ask students to get out their notebooks. Today students will add solutions to complete the Character/Setting/Problem structures they set up the day before. This strategy gives students an opportunity to see where the story is headed. It enables them to work with the story's structure and to know the end before they begin writing. Of course, it's important to let students know that they may revise their ending at any time. This CSP chart simply gives them valuable direction.

First, we add the solutions to the CSPs we wrote as a class. When we finish, our class chart looks like this.

C — A boy
S — The playground
P — Someone is making fun of him.
s — He goes to the guidance counselor and she helps him.

C — A grandpa and grandma
S — A farmhouse
P — The house catches on fire.
s — The neighbors help them rebuild.

C — A puppy
S — A neighborhood
P — The puppy is lost.
s — The puppy is found at the pound.

Students love working with CSPs. If they keep them in their notebooks, then ready-made story structures are at their fingertips when they're searching for an idea.

Sample of Student Work

C — Little Red Riding Hood

S — The woods and grandmother's house

P — Wolf wants to eat Little Red Riding Hood

1 — Goes to Wolf Shopping Center

2 — Goes to Grandma's and puts her in the closet

3 — Wolf tries to trick Little Red Riding Hood

s — Grandmother finds a broom in a closet and sweeps the wolf away.

Strategy: Teach Students to Arrive at a Fictional Ending

If writers understand basic storytelling structure, they will have a better idea how to reach the end of the stories they write. Here we'll look at one very basic, but very common story structure. If students are familiar with this structure, they can use it in their own stories.

Focus Lesson 2: Focus on Story Structure

For this lesson, you will need a book that closely follows this basic story structure—character, setting, problem, three attempts to solve the problem, and the solution. A perfect book for this lesson is *Wolf!* by Becky Bloom. Before you read this book aloud, place students in groups of three, four, or five. The first group will listen for the character, the second group will listen for the setting, the third for the problem, the fourth for the three ways to solve the problem, and the fifth will listen for the solution. Listening for a purpose encourages students to listen closely and actively. This lesson also allows students to interact with one another. You will need a premade chart that lists: *Title, Characters, Setting, Problem, Event 1, Event 2, Event 3,* and *Solution.*

Read the story with expression. After reading, ask students to supply the story elements listed on the chart. Record their responses. For the story *Wolf!*, the chart should look something like this:

Characters: A wolf, a pig, a cow, a duck

Setting: A farm outside a little town

Problem: The pig, cow, and duck can read. The wolf can't.

Event 1:	The wolf goes to school, but that doesn't help because the animals aren't impressed.
Event 2:	The wolf goes to the public library and reads, studies, and practices. The animals think he has improved, but he needs to work on his style.
Event 3:	The wolf goes to the bookshop and buys his own book. He keeps reading and practicing.
Solution:	The wolf reads with confidence and passion. He reads so well that the pig, cow, and duck want him to keep reading stories. The animals decide they could become storytellers and travel the world. But the wolf is happy just to have wonderful friends.

Once you have presented this lesson, encourage students to look for other literature that follows the same pattern. A great many do. The more exposure students have to story structure, the more organized and fluent their writing becomes. As the writing becomes more concise, you will notice that the rambling slowly disappears. Beginnings are difficult, but endings are more difficult when students don't know where they are headed, at least in the early years. In order to write an effective ending, students need to understand the process from beginning to end. Once writers internalize the basic structures, it is easier for them to work on some of the other important writing traits, such as fluency, voice, strong vocabulary, and elaboration.

Strategy: Help Students See the Relationship Between the Story's Problem and Its Ending

In a well-crafted story, the main character takes ownership of the problem. That ownership spawns the reader's interest in the outcome of the story. The reader longs to find out how the character solves the problem. If the writer doesn't understand structure, he or she will not be able to craft an effective ending. Young writers especially will get lost and lose their focus.

Something else we can observe in most effective short stories is that the problem is made clear very early on. Think back to *The Beast in the Bathtub*, in which the problem was stated in the very first line. Making the problem apparent early on is another way to win the reader's interest and sympathy.

Focus Lesson 3: State the Problem Early and Make Sure the Main Character Solves It

To begin this lesson, return to Becky Bloom's *Wolf!* and invite students to listen again to the story.

Mrs. H-D:	Writers, when you write fiction, it is important to introduce the problem as close to the beginning as possible. That helps to capture the reader's attention. It is just as important for the main character to solve his or her own problem. Now we know the wolf is the main character. As I reread the story, I'd like you to listen carefully for the point in the story where the wolf takes charge. (*Read the story.*)

Mrs. H-D:	Who can tell me when the wolf took charge?
Molly:	Right after we found out the problem.
Mrs. H-D:	What is the problem?
Jared:	The animals ignore the wolf and he can't read.
Mrs. H-D:	I'd like someone to explain how the wolf took charge.
Landon:	He started solving his problem. He went to school, the library, and then he bought his own book. He also practiced. A lot!
Mrs. H-D:	How would it change the story if the pig, cow, or duck solved the wolf's problem?
Jill:	I don't think it would be interesting.
Mrs. H-D:	Please explain.
Jill:	I like the way the wolf kept trying. He just kept trying to get better. The wolf is like me. When I couldn't multiply, I kept practicing.
Rob:	Lots of people like to solve their own problems.
Mrs. H-D:	You are exactly right.
Rob:	Writing the end would be harder. This way, I could think of things the wolf would do because I would think of how I would solve the problem.
Mrs. H-D:	I agree. It is important to have the main character solve the problem. If the pig tried to solve the wolf's problem, the story would have lost focus. Pretty soon the pig's own problems would pop up in the story and the author would have been trying to solve more than one problem. It's equally important to present the problem near the beginning.

Writers, if you are working on a fictional story, I'd like you to reread it now. With a highlighter mark the place where the problem is introduced. Remember to keep the problem close to the beginning. Next, highlight the point in your story where the main character takes charge and begins to solve his or her own problem. If you find there is another character or force that is in charge, you will need to revise. When our writing time has ended and you have given this strategy a try, please sign up to share.

Sample of Student Work

Worried Willie

Worried Willie is always worried. He has black hair and blue eyes. His favorite color is green. There once was a story of a boy. His name was Willie, but most people called him Worried Willie. He always worries, no matter what. He worried about monsters, cats, and dogs. One day he went to school. Willie went to his new desk and he looked in it. Willie saw eyes. Willie screamed, Ahhhh Help! Mr. Black looked in Willie's desk. It was the classes pet rabbit. Whew that was a close one! said Willie. He worried the rest of the day about the rabbit because he thought that the rabbit would come back. On his math he got an F because he worried and got no work done.

When school was out, Willie ran home as fast as he could. He was worried that he would run out of breath... and do you know what? He ran out of breath. Noooooo! he yelled. He thought he would be stuck in town forever. Help me, he yelled. He went to call his mom. After Willie got home he went to his room and worried until night. Soon he was tired so he tried to get sleep but then he saw something moving. It was his pet dog, Ahhhh he screamed! He ran over to his window and jumped out his window. Crash! Right into a trash can. When he got out he was perfectly fine. The next day he went to school and do you know what? He didn't worry about anything, not even mosters, cats, and dogs. And that's the story of Worried Willie.

Strategy: Teach Students the Importance of Logical Endings

If our students understand the basics of plot, they will be more able to compose solutions and logical endings. Though it isn't always readily apparent, with a little scrutiny, you'll see that there are some very basic plots that show up again and again in stories.

Focus Lesson 4: Beginning to End—Understanding Plot

In this lesson, introduce students to several common plot types. For instance, in Margory Cuyler's book, *Freckles and Willie,* the plot is boy meets girl, but then the two encounter a problem. Another basic plot is lost and found. An example of a lost-and-found plot is Vera Rosenberry's *Vera Runs Away.* Vera runs away and her family finds her. The plot of *Ridiculous* by Michael Coleman consists of a character struggling with nature. A tortoise tries find out about winter by staying awake. *Wemberly Worried* by Kevin Henkes is an example of a plot where the character has a personal problem that she works to solve.

Although many pieces of literature contain more than one plot, for our students, a single plot suffices. Read alouds, guided reading, and shared reading are excellent opportunities to teach these basic plots. Whenever teaching plot, help students remember the word *struggle*. The main character struggles in each of the plots mentioned above. The struggle in a plot needn't be earth-shattering, but it has be meaningful to the character in the story.

Once students grasp plot, the next step is to teach them how to solve the problem. I encourage teachers to use threes. The number three has traditionally had great significance. For writers who are describing characters struggling to overcome a problem, three is the perfect number; if the character succeeds on the second try, the effort does not seem great enough, and no tension is built. Four tries, on the other hand, can begin to feel like too much.

Suggest to students that they have their main character attempt three times to solve the problem they face. The first two times the character tries and fails. The third time, the character succeeds.

Let's look again at *Wolf!* In this story, the wolf went to school. But his first attempt wasn't enough. The wolf doesn't give up, however. He tries again. Admirably, he runs to the public library. And he studies hard. Still it's not enough; the animals feel he needs to work on his style. In each of the first two events, the tension increases. But still the wolf doesn't give up. He tries one more time. This allows him to build confidence. Finally, on this third attempt, the wolf succeeds. The animals love the passion the wolf reads with. In fact, they are so impressed, they keep asking him to read one story after the other. That leads to the solution. The animals will all become storytellers and travel the world. Yet, the wolf is just happy to have good friends.

Both beginnings and endings are vital to a well-written story. Expect students to struggle with endings, but helping them understand plot will help them write effective endings.

Sample of Student Work

The Three Pigs

Once upon a time there lived three little pigs. The older one's name was David. The middle one's name was Evan. The little one's name was Jack. They were all thinking about building a house. So, one day they went down to the piggy mart. The first one got dirt. The second got sticks. And the third one had a stone house. When they got out of the piggy mart they went to the forest. They had all the tools they needed. Then they started building. It took them 3 hours. They they were done. They turned on the television. Right when they turned it on it said there had been a fox invasion in piggy woods. So, all pigs lock your door. So, the fox doesn't come. All the pigs locked there doors. But, in one hour the fox came to Jack's house. Let me in, Let me in. Let me in. No, No, No, not by the hair of my precious tail. Well I'll hugg and I'll puff and I'll blow your house down. Whooooosh, Whooooosh, Whooooosh, aaaaaaa said Jack I better get to Evan's house. O man. I lost a pig again. So, the fox went to Evan's house. Whooooosh, Whooooosh, Whooooosh and the house came down. aaaaaaa they both said and they ran to David's house. The fox said Let me in, Let me in. No, No, No, Not by the hair of my precious tail. Then I'll huff and I'll puff and I'll blow your house down. Whooooosh, Whooooosh, Whooooosh, I'll give one more chance. Whooooosh. Ha, Ha, Ha, I knew you couldn't said David. I'll never bother you again said the fox. Bye said the fox. See ya. said the three little pigs. That's why we don't have any fox.

Chapter 3 Review

- Teach basic story structures.
- Give students practice mapping out stories using Character/Setting/Problem/Solution (CSPs).
- Encourage students to state the story's problem early and have the main character solve it.

Chapter 4

Crafting Nonfiction Endings

An effective ending brings closure. This is true whether you are writing fiction or nonfiction. Many of the same fictional endings may be used to end nonfiction pieces. For instance, a story may have a circular ending, and so may nonfiction. A story may end with a thought or a question, and so may nonfiction.

When teaching students to craft nonfiction endings, the first thing I encourage teachers and students to do is to visit the school library or to explore their own classroom libraries. Once again, look at how published writers of nonfiction end their pieces. I also encourage teachers to read the advice of seasoned writing teachers such as Ralph Fletcher, William Zinsser, and Donald Graves. Read aloud to students the advice of the professionals on topics such as beginnings, endings, and voice. Post large charts with quotes from famous writers for students to refer to. Then try the following lessons to deepen students' understanding of nonfiction endings.

Strategy: Teach Students to Recognize Balance When Writing a Nonfiction Ending

Beginnings and endings should be in balance with each other. As we discussed in the last chapter, many nonfiction books, especially books that deliver information, make the reader a promise in the beginning. We expect that the ending of these books will "clinch" this promise. I use the word *balance* to suggest that the ending should in some way demonstrate an awareness of the promise made up front. This is not a circular ending, but an ending that follows through on the promise made at the beginning.

Focus Lesson 1: Are the Beginning and Ending in Balance?

To explore this aspect of balance in the ending of a nonfiction book, I choose Seymour Simon's *Cats*. On large chart paper, I write Simon's introduction and conclusion for the students. I want them to focus on whether there is balance between the beginning and the ending. Please listen in.

Mrs. H-D: Writers, this morning we are going to look at how to write an effective ending for the informational animal book you have been writing. When writers write an informational introduction, they write with a main idea. I like to call it a "promise." Let's look at Seymour Simon's introduction to his information book about cats. (*We read this together.*) Who can tell me what the main idea is on this page? (It is promise.)

Brandon: I think it is the last sentence when he says that if you learn about cats, it will help you select a pet cat and take care of it.

Mrs. H-D: You are correct, Brandon. Now, let's think about the type of information you might find in this book.

Adam: How to take care of a cat.

James: I think he will tell us about all the different kinds of cats.

Mrs. H-D: One more idea, please.

Jenna: I think we will learn about the things cats like to do.

Mrs. H-D: When a writer crafts an ending, he or she creates a balance by referring in some way back to the beginning. That helps the writer to bring closure to his piece. Let's see if Seymour Simon does that for you. Let's read the ending together. (*We read the ending.*)

Brandon: I think Seymour Simon kept his promise. His beginning and ending are balanced because in his introduction he said that learning about a cat can help you pick a cat, and in the end he says that for many people, cats make great pets. He doesn't say for all people. The more you know about cats and the way they are, the better choice you'll make about getting a cat for a pet.

Mrs. H-D: Your response is very reflective, Brandon. This morning, writers, I would like you to carefully read the beginning to the information book you're writing. Ask yourself what the main idea is in your introduction. What did you promise your audience? Then I want you to reread your ending. Ask yourself if your writing balanced. Did you bring the reader to a satisfying conclusion by keeping your promise? Be prepared to share what you learned about your writing.

Sample of Student Work

The Rainforest by Spencer

Would you like to visit the rainforest some day? Read the following interesting facts and decide for yourself.

The rainforest has really slimy things and moss. It has rivers and trees with monkeys hanging on the limbs. The monkeys in the rainforest throw mangoes.

The Amazon River is in half of the rainforests in the world. The Amazon River is 4,000 miles long. That is long.

The rainforest has army ants in it. There are snakes and crocodiles in the river. It is misty in the rainforest and there are tall trees. It rains a lot in the rainforest.

The rainforest is fascinating. There is so much we can learn from the rainforest. I would be afraid to go to the rainforest. Don't ask me why, because I don't know. Would you like to visit the rainforest?

Strategy: Teach Students to Reassure Their Audience

Many nonfiction topics are new and unfamiliar to students. While I was researching endings for nonfiction writing, I discovered something interesting. I found that in many titles written about weather and animals, both of which can be intimidating to some students, the author actually concludes the piece with an ending that is reassuring to the reader.

Focus Lesson 2: End with Reassurance

The following is the lesson I presented to my students after making the discovery noted above.

Mrs. H-D: Writers, this morning I would like to share with you something I noticed writers do when they write about topics that might be scary and dangerous. Let's look at the way three authors ended their nonfiction pieces. The three books we are going to take a look at are Jim Arnosky's *Rattlesnakes*, *Earthquakes* by Seymour Simon, and *Do Tornadoes Really Twist? Questions and Answers About Tornadoes and Hurricanes* by Melva and Gilda Berger. *(I've made overheads of the three different endings.)* I'm going to read each one to you and I'd like you to tell me something you noticed that is similar about these three endings. *(I read* Earthquakes *first.)*

It also helps to know what to do when an earthquake strikes. If you are indoors, get under a heavy table, desk, or bed. Stay away form windows, mirrors, or high cabinets. If you are in a high building, stay out of the elevators and stairways. If you are outdoors, move away from high buildings, walls, power polls, or any other tall objects. If possible, move to an open area. Above all, remain calm and don't worry. The chances of your being hurt in a quake are very, very slight.

(Next, I read Do Tornadoes Really Twist? Questions and Answers About Tornadoes and Hurricanes.*)*

Do hurricanes do any good?
   Yes. In spite of the destruction they cause, hurricanes help maintain the heat balance throughout the world. The heavy winds help carry heat from the tropics to the polar regions. Like a safety valve, hurricanes release excess energy and spread it out. Hurricane rains also bring lots of fresh water for crops and replenish groundwater.

(Finally, I read Jim Arnosky's Rattlesnakes.*)*

The greatest threat to rattlesnakes comes from us. When we bulldoze and build in rattlesnake habitat, we drive the snakes out and crowd them onto less and less land. Some people, fearful of rattlesnakes, destroy every one they see. Rattlesnakes are scary and dangerous, but they are also beautiful and highly efficient predators of small animals, especially rodents. Rattlesnakes deserve all the room and respect we can give them – for their well-being and for ours.

Tia: I noticed the endings are all good.

Mrs. H-D: What do you mean by good?

Tia: The endings are positive. Some people might be afraid of earthquakes, hurricanes, and rattlesnakes, but the author also tells us something good about each of these things. For example, an earthquake might damage a lot of things, but the chances of me being in an earthquake are very small. The author made me feel safe.

Mrs. H-D: Tia, you are right on track. I noticed the same thing. I named this a "reassuring" ending. Each of the authors ended with something positive, which reassures us as readers that we don't have to be fearful. We need to have both knowledge and respect for our environment. There is good and bad in many things.

Jason: That's what my dad says about the world.

Mrs. H-D: Writers, this morning I would like you to read through the nonfiction pieces you've been writing and see if somewhere in your writing you could try a reassuring ending. Good luck!

Sample of Student Work

The Rainforest by Spencer (Revised Ending Paragraph)

I would be afraid to go to the rainforest. Don't ask me why, because I don't know. Maybe someday I'll change my mind, because the rainforest has fascinating animals, plants, and trees. There is so much everyone can learn from studying the rainforest. Would you like to visit the rainforest?

Strategy: Teach Students to End With Informational Notes

When I came across the book *The Birds in My Barn* by Kathleen Hardcastle Moeller, I knew I wanted to use this book to teach my second-grade students how to end their narrative pieces in a completely different way. This book teaches students to combine personal narrative and informational text. The story begins in the early morning when the young boy visits the barn. He sees that a wren has built a nest in the horse's blanket. Later in the morning he sees a red cardinal at the stall window. Later still, he notices bluebirds flying across the meadow. At noon he sees a crow as he eats his lunch beneath a tree. In mid-afternoon he watches a mockingbird. Late in the day, mourning doves coo all around him. At the end of the narrative, there is a picture of an owl. There are a couple of things I could teach with this text. I could teach students to write a narrative that begins in the morning and ends at night. But it is the end of the book that I feel is most important. Katie Moeller ends the book with informational notes. Referring back to the cover and pages where each bird is introduced, she gives the reader information about each bird the young boy saw.

Focus Lesson 3: Write a Personal Narrative That Ends with Informational Notes.

It just so happened that my class had scheduled a learning trip to the zoo, which gave me a great opportunity to give this lesson. But you can take a class nature walk, or perhaps give students the "homework" of observing their surroundings for an afternoon, armed with a pen and notebook. Your students can be fact finders anywhere—at the park, the grocery store, or a bustling ice-cream shop on a Saturday afternoon.

On the day of the trip, each student was supplied with a little spiral notebook and pen. I asked students to record the animals they saw at the zoo and jot down some interesting facts. When we returned, I read them the book and we made a criteria chart. Let's listen in.

Mrs. H-D: I'd like you to try writing a personal narrative about our learning trip to the zoo. I'd also like you to end your writing with informational notes. You may use your spiral notebooks to help you. But first, I'm going to read you an example of a personal narrative with informational notes. Then we will make a criteria chart to help you with your writing.

I typed the text on an overhead so they have a visual example to refer back to when I'm finished reading. Next I read the text aloud. When I'm finished reading, there is a large chart labeled Personal Narrative With Informational Notes Criteria Chart.

Mrs. H-D: Writers, share with us some of the quality things you noticed about Kathleen Moeller's writing that you might want to include in your piece about our learning trip to the zoo.

As the students respond, I write their responses on the criteria chart.

Jenna: She moved time by beginning in the morning and ending at night. We could do the same thing with our writing.

Mrs. H-D: Good point, Jenna. Someone else.

Rachel: She used lots of similes like her nest was *as round as a little bowl* and her eggs *as small as pebbles*.

Nik: She used strong verbs like *dazzled, perched,* and *flashed*.

Personal Narrative with Informational Criteria Chart

- Moves time
- Use simile
- Strong verbs
- A beginning, middle, and end
- Rich details
- Sound
- Informational notes—information and page number
- Uses alliteration

Mrs. H-D: And those verbs are important.

Desmond: She has a beginning, middle, and end and she used rich details.

Mrs. H-D: Share with us the details that really stick with you. The ones you wish you wrote.

Desmond: I liked the part when she was writing about the cardinal and said, "I saw a little red flag fluttering at the stall window."

Angela: She uses some alliteration like *brilliant blue*.

Nik: She used sound when she wrote about the crows. *Caw-caw-caw*.

Mrs. H-D: How about when she ends with the informational notes?

Angela: I noticed she includes the page number and then the information.

Desmond: There are lots of examples when she writes her information.

Mrs. H-D: Say more.

Desmond: Like when she tells about the places a house wren builds its house, she says in old shoes, hats, and mailboxes, and even in the pocket of clothing left outside.

Adele: In the notes, the author is descriptive, uses alliteration, rich details and many of the same things as she used in the first part of the book.

Mrs. H-D: Writers, I'm so proud of you! You are talking like writers providing the class with strong writing qualities and specific examples. Now, I'd like you to get started with your pieces. Make sure you end your piece with informational notes.

The activities I've described in Chapters 1 and 2 are just a few to get you going on your own exploration of leads and endings with your students. Let his book be a springboard for discovering even more ways to help your students to create effective beginnings and endings. Every piece of writing is unique, and every lead and ending will be unique too. But we can help our students follow some common guidelines to help them express themselves and their stories more fully.

Conferencing and sharing are two more tools that will bolster the writers in your classroom.

Chapter 4 Review

- Introduce a variety of nonfiction endings.
- Help students balance their endings with their beginnings.
- Have students experiment with different types of endings.

Chapter 5

Conferencing and Sharing

Powerful Tools

The focus lessons I present in previous chapters give students the tools they need to write effective beginnings and endings. But uninterrupted writing time is necessary for students to be able to put those tools to use and integrate them into their own writing repertoire. I advocate providing one hour of writing workshop daily, so teachers have time to offer direct instruction through focus lessons and mini lessons and so students have plenty of time to write.

Conferring and sharing are invaluable components of writing instruction as well. The one-on-one teaching that take place during a conference enables teachers to meet the needs of each individual in the class. Having students share their work and respond to the work of others helps them feel part of a real writing community and provides specific feedback from an authentic audience. In this chapter, I will explore these two aspects of teaching writing and demonstrate how they can support students as they develop their ability to write effective beginnings and endings.

Conferencing

One of the most important ways to help students with their writing is through conferencing. Conferencing can be done with the teacher or a peer. It takes lots of practice on the part of the classroom teacher to conference effectively. Furthermore, peer conferencing requires lots of modeling by the classroom teacher. If you are interested in learning more about conferencing, I recommend Carl Anderson's *How's It Going?*

The most important thing to keep in mind with any piece of student writing is that it is the child's writing, not yours. When I first started writing workshop, I caught myself giving students my ideas. I remember a writer who didn't know how to end his story. So what did I do? I gave him my idea rather than gently nudging the student through effective questioning, or taking the time to gather books by professional authors and have him explore the kind of ending that would be appropriate for his particular piece. When

I gave him my idea, he not only lost ownership, but I deprived him of the opportunity to be an independent learner.

Through lots of practice, I've become better at conferencing. I've learned to nudge instead of suggest. When I conference with students, I pull up a student chair and sit at eye level with them. The following is a conference I had with Brandon. Brandon is imaginative. He has a passion for nonfiction and fantasy.

Mrs. H-D: How's it going, Brandon?

Brandon: Good.

Mrs. H-D: Tell me a little about your piece.

Brandon: I'm writing about dolphins and whales. I'm finished.

Mrs. H-D: Would you like to read your piece to me? If you want I'll read it to you.

Brandon: I'll read it to you. Will you listen and tell me if it makes sense?

Mrs. H-D: Sure.

At this point, Brandon reads his piece to me. He has lots of information. He's used strong verbs, and his writing is fluent. There are two things I notice. One is that he doesn't have a beginning.

The other is he ends this piece with "Good-Bye!" During this time I need to decide what I'm going to address . . . the beginning or the end. I only choose one teaching point because I don't want to overwhelm Brandon. Hopefully when Brandon shares with the class, someone will suggest that he needs to write a more appropriate ending.

Dolphins are Whales

Dolphins are mammals. So are whales. Dolphins are close cousins to the whales. People once said that whales lived on land and their back flippers, and front flippers were legs, but that's just a myth. Whales are not fish because they don't have gills. Gills are lines that have slits. The slits take the water's oxegyn in and squirt out the water through the gill slits. Whales use blowholes. The blowhole opens when the whale is breathing on the surface of the water, but when they go under the water it closes. A shark only feeds on baby whales. Because a full grown whale is too big for a shark to fight it. But if a whale's mom, or, dad sees the baby getting attacked, the mom, or, dad will call for the herd. The herd of whales circle the shark. Then they would scare the shark away. Sharks mainly don't mess with whales. Because whales put up a pretty good fight. Whalers used to hunt blue whales. But they began to die out. So it became a law not to hunt blue whales. Because if blue whales were still to be hunted the blue whale would be extinct. When a whale jumps from the water and makes a big splash this is called breaching. There are two groups of whales. Toothed whales, and baleen whales. A whale can't be under the water for seven hours. A whale can only be under water for one hour. A dolphin can only be under water for twenty-three minutes. Mother whales take care of their calfs for 3 years. This is called nursing.

When a new dolphin, or, whale calf is born in the pack as fast as they can they need to push the calf to the surface for it's first breath. A *dolphin calf is nursed for 2 years. Whales feed on tiny plants or animals called plankton. Dolphins feed on fish. And whales sometimes eat little animals called krill. GOOD-BYE!*

Mrs. H-D: Brandon, where did you get all this information about whales and dolphins?

Brandon: I read books. We have lots of books about sea animals at our house.

Mrs. H-D: Your information is organized and it makes sense. I'd like you to help me with something? Who is your audience?

Brandon: People who like whales and dolphins.

Mrs. H-D: Can you think of a way to capture the attention of the people who like whales and dolphins?

Brandon: I could ask them in the beginning.

Mrs. H-D: How might you do that?

Brandon: I'm not sure. I'll have to think.

Mrs. H-D: Brandon, I'm going to conference with Nik now. If you come up with something, I'd like you to share it with the class. Good luck!

When writing time was over, Brandon tapped on my shoulder and said, "I have a beginning. May I share?" The following is Brandon's beginning.

Do you want to come with me on a fact filled adventure? Well then come, follow me.

When he read it, I smiled. His beginning not only had a sense of audience, it had Brandon's voice!

Sharing Time

Sharing time is another way to help student writers improve their writing. During sharing time, the author sits in a special chair and reads his or her piece to the class. Third- and fourth-grade students should be given the opportunity to set a purpose for the audience. In other words, the author might ask the audience to listen for meaning, sentence fluency, or whether the piece has a captivating beginning or a satisfying ending. The other members of the classroom writing community become the audience. The responsibility of the audience is to listen, respond, and question. If students are having a difficult time providing their full attention, I tell them to focus on the author's lips. When students watch the author's lips, it helps them to focus on what is being said.

> With younger students, I write the questions on a sticky note. Fourth graders should be asked to write their own responses. That way, the notes can be given to the author and he or she can stick the questions on their piece of writing.

After the author finishes reading the piece, the audience is required to provide three appreciations. Appreciations are responses in which the members of the audience tell the author something they have done well. When a student says "I like your story," that is not an appreciation, unless the student has said something like this, "I like your story because you used strong verbs like *squirt, attack,* and *circle.*" Children need to learn to talk like writers. Appreciations need to be specific. When students do this, you'll know they were listening and so will the writer.

Next, the audience is asked to respond to the writer with three questions or suggestions. The questions should be specific and they should make the writing stronger. If a student asks, "How old is the boy's dad?" and the age of the dad does not improve the quality of the story, then you need to respond to the child like this: "Tell us how you think the dad's age is going to help this story." We need to make students accountable. Maybe the student has a very good reason for asking the question. But the writing community will not know unless the student is held responsible for the question.

> The student author should be in charge. He or she asks the students for appreciations and questions. At this point, the teacher becomes a part of the audience raising his or her hand like the rest of the students.

Another strategy students can use is to ask the author to help them understand or to explain. Discourage the use of the phrase, "You should." It is important that we keep our classroom writing communities safe. If we accomplish this, all children will feel free to share. All students accept appreciations and all students accept critical feedback. Students want their writing to improve and the writing community has a responsibility to help each member.

How do we encourage students to talk like writers and critique like writers? The answer is simple. You provide the model. You become an integral part of the classroom writing community. When the audience extends appreciations, you extend appreciations. When the audience questions, or asks for explanations, you respond accordingly. The best advice I can offer is to MODEL, MODEL, MODEL! You will be pleasantly surprised at how your students learn to respond in a meaningful and sophisticated way.

The following is an example of a share time held in my second-grade classroom. The child who is sharing loves nonfiction. Read the following carefully.

Mrs. H-D: Nik, please go to the author's chair. We are ready. Is there anything you would like the audience to specifically listen for?

Nik: No.

At this point Nik reads his story.

> *Oh the wonders what you can learn about in Australia's Animals, a book about Australia's Animals by Nik*
>
> *Australia has a whole lot of animals. Australia has 9 of the most venomous snakes in the world and they all come out at night. And crocodiles are almost invisible in the river in the day. And the rock wallaby is like a pogo stick on the rocks. And a frilled lizard has a frill to spread around his head toward predators. Kangaroos use their big back legs to hop very quickly. Iguanas will eat mice and sometimes other lizards. A male platypus has claws on its ankles that are poisonous, too. Dingo dogs are wild dogs that live in Australia, and the kookaburra is a loud bird. They are mostly in the trees or they are flying in the air.*

After Nik reads his story, the audience responds as follows:

Mrs. H-D: Who has an appreciation?

Maddy: I appreciate the information you gave us.

Mrs. H-D: Please be more specific. Tell Nik what you learned.

Maddy: I didn't know iguanas eat mice.

Mrs. H-D: Another appreciation.

Landon: I appreciate your strong vocabulary like *venomous* and *invisible*.

Mrs. H-D: One more appreciation from the student audience.

Daniel: I appreciate when you said the rock wallaby is like a pogo stick. I think you wrote a simile.

Mrs. H-D: I appreciate you were listening closely. Otherwise you may not have caught the simile.

Mrs. H-D: Nik, I appreciate the way you kept your focus on Australian animals. Now, who has a question or suggestion?

David: You have a good title. You might want to use part of that for a beginning.

Nik: Thanks. I'll think about that.

Haley: You might add an ending. Your writing stops with the kookaburra. I suggest adding a summary or thought.

Nik: I was going to do that.

Mrs. H-D: We need one more question or suggestion from the student audience.

Audrey: A lot of your sentences begin with *and*. You might want to leave some of those *ands* out.

Nik: Thanks. I'll think about that.

Mrs. H-D: Nik, I agree with the suggestion about the title. You might want to think about ending your piece circling back to the hook.

Nik: Thanks Mrs. H.-Dove. That's what I was thinking.

> If students don't respond, wait. Do not come to their rescue. Someone will come up with an appreciation, question, or suggestion. If you come to the rescue, students will always expect that. If your expectation is higher than theirs, someone will always rise to the top.

Below you will find Nik's new ending. Notice, he did not address all of the audience's suggestions. But look at his ending. I'm sure he borrowed it from a television program, yet I celebrate Nik's attempt to leave us with an ending that not only satisfies, but invites us to look forward to the next piece of his writing.

- Think about using the title for the beginning
- Are you planning on adding an ending?
- You might think about varying your sentence beginnings.

Nik's new ending

I have told you a whole lot but now our time is up. So I will see you next time on Oh the Wonders what you can learn about Australia's Animals.

Conferring and sharing are important parts of writing instruction, and I highly recommend they become an integral part of your teaching. Focusing on beginnings and endings during this time is natural, and students often revise one or the other based on comments they receive during a conference or share time.

A Final Reflection

As I reread this book there was one thing that stood out that made me proud to be a teacher of young writers. If you noticed during the many lessons presented, I didn't always say a lot. But the conversations the students participated in were rich. Students discussed book titles, quality writing, and expressed ideas. The conversations represent a classroom community of writers—students who respect and help each other. I'm grateful to all those students who participated in the many writing communities with me. They taught me so much about children, writing, and teaching.

Bibliography

Adler, David A. *The Babe and I.* Orlando: Voyager Books. Harcourt, Inc., 1999.

Anderson, Carl. *How's It Going?: A Practical Guide for Conferring with Student Writers.* Portsmouth, N.H: Heinemann, 2000.

Armstrong, William H. *Sounder.* New York: Harper Juvenile,1989.

Arnosky, Jim. *All About Rattlesnakes.* New York: Scholastic, 1997.

Arnosky, Jim. *All About Sharks.* New York: Scholastic, 2003.

Bang, Molly. *When Sophie Gets Angry—Really, Really Angry.* New York: Scholastic, 1999.

Barbour, Karen. *Little Nino's Pizzeria.* San Diego: Voyager Books, 1987.

Bauer, Marion Dane. *What's Your Story?: A Young Person's Guide to Writing Fiction.* New York: Clarion Books, 1992.

Berger, Melvin and Gilda. *Do Tornadoes Really Twist? Questions and Answers About Tornadoes and Hurricanes.* New York: Scholastic, 2000.

Blaine, Marge. *The Terrible Thing That Happened At Our House.* New York: Scholastic, 1975.

Bloom, Becky. *Wolf!* New York: Orchard Books, 1999.

Burleigh, Robert. *Home Run.* San Diego: Voyager Books. Harcourt, Inc., 1998.

Coleman, Michael. *Ridiculous.* Wauwatosa, WI: Little Tiger Press, 1996.

Crews, Donald. *Shortcut.* New York: Mulberry Books, 1992.

Cuyler, Margery. *Freckles and Willie.* New York: Henry Holt and Company, 1986.

DiCamillo, Kate. *Because of Winn-Dixie.* New York: Scholastic, 2000.

Diestel-Fedderson, Mary. *Try Again Sally Jane.* Milwaukee: Gareth Stevens Publishing, 1987.

Gray, Libba Moore. *Dear Willie Rudd,.* New York: Alladin Paperbacks, 2000.

Gray, Libba Moore. *My Mama Had a Dancing Heart.* New York: Orchard Books, 1995.

Heide, Florence Parry. *Some Things are Scary.* Cambridge: Candlewick Press, 2000.

Henkes, Kevin. *Wemberly Worried.* New York: Scholastic, 2000.

Hoose, Phillip and Hannah. *Hey, Little Ant.* Berkeley, California: Tricycle Press, 1998.

Hopkinson, Deborah. *Bluebird Summer.* Singapore: Greenwillow Books, 2001.

Huliska-Beith, Laura. *The Book of Bad Ideas.* Boston: Little, Brown and Company, 2000.

Ketteman, Helen. *I Remember Papa.* New York: Dial Books for Young Readers, 1998.

Lesser, Carolyn. *The Goodnight Circle.* San Diego: Harcourt Brace Jovanovich, Publishers, 1984.

Levine, Sarah and Abby. *Sometimes I Wish I Were Mindy.* Niles, Illinois: Albert Whitman & Company, 1986.

Littlesugar, Amy. *Freedom School, Yes!* New York: Philomel Books, 2001.

McLerran, Alice. *Roxaboxen.* New York: Scholastic, 1991.

Moeller, Kathleen Hardcastle. *The Birds at My Barn.* Katonah, N.Y.: Richard C. Owens Publishers, Inc., 2000.

Moore, Elaine. *Grandma's Smile.* New York: Lothrop, Lee & Shepard Books, 1995.

Morrissey, Dean. *The Monster Trap.* New York: Harper Collins Publishers, 2004.

Munsch, Robert. *The Paper Bag Princess.* Toronto: Annick Press LTD., 1991.

Numeroff, Laura. *If You Give a Pig a Pancake.* New York: HarperCollins Children's Books, 1998.

Peterson, Esther A. *Frederick's Alligator.* New York: Crown Publishers, Inc., 1997.

Pinkwater, Daniel. *I Was A Second Grade Werewolf.* New York: E.P. Dutton, 1983.

Polacco, Patricia. *Mr. Lincoln's Way.* New York: Philomel Books, 2001.

Ray, Katie Wood. *Wondrous Words: Writers and Writing in the Elementary Classroom.* USA: National Council of Teachers of English, 1999.

Rosenberry, Vera. *Vera Runs Away.* New York: Henry Holt and Company, 2000.

Rylant, Cynthia. *The Relatives Came.* New York: Alladin Paperbacks, 1985.

Simon, C. "A Long Wait." *Click.* Vol. 3, May/June 2000.

Simon, Seymour. *Cats.* New York: Scholastic, 2004.

Simon, Seymour. *Earthquakes.* New York: Scholastic, 1991.

Small, David. *Ruby Mae Has Something to Say.* New York: Crown Publishers Inc., 1992.

Stevens, Janet and Susan Stevens Crummel. *Cook-A-Doodle-Doo!* Harcourt Brace & Company: San Diego, 1999.

Stevens, Kathleen. *The Beast in the Bathtub.* Milwaukee: Gareth Stevens, Inc.,1985.

Schwartz, Amy. *Bea and Mr. Jones.* New York: Penguin Books, 1982.

Van Riper Jr., Guernsey. *Babe Ruth: One of Baseball's Greatest.* New York: Aladdin Paperbacks, 1954.

Vyner, Sue and Tim. *The Stolen Egg.* New York: Viking, 1992.

Willems, Mo. *The Pigeon Finds a Hot Dog!* New York: Hyperion Books, 2004.

Wood, Audrey. *The Red Racer.* New York: Simon & Schuster, 1996.

Woodson, Jacqueline. *The Other Side.* New York: G.P. Putnam's Sons, 2001.

Yolen, Jane. *Miz Berlin Walks.* New York: Puffin Books, 1997.

Yolen, Jane. *Moon Ball.* New York: Puffin Books, 1997.

Yolen, Jane. *Sleeping Ugly.* New York: Scholastic, 1992.

Zolotow, Charlotte. *The Seashore Book.* New York: Harper Collins Publishers, 1992.

Rosswurm, V. "Exotic animals not the best choice for family pets." Auburn, Indiana: *The Evening Star*, July 24, 2005.